A Certain Magical
D0888561
27
CHUYA KOGINO
ORIGINAL STORY:
KAZUMA KAMACHI
CHARACTER DESIGN:
KIYOTAKA HAIMURA

A CERTAIN MAGICAL INDEX 27 TABLE OF CONTENTS

Index Librorum Prohibitorum

#162 SAINTBREAKER ⑤

SEEKING SALVATION FROM THE WEAK...

IT'S TRUE THAT MY COMRADES HAVE BEEN HURT JUST FOR BEING AT MY SIDE.
I WAS AFRAID IT WOULD HAPPEN AGAIN, SO I TRIED TO DISTANCE MYSELF FROM THE AMAKUSA CHURCH...
HOW-EVER ...
...SUCH TRAGEDIES DIDN'T HAPPEN BECAUSE OF ANY WEAKNESS ON THEIR PART.
I WAS THE ONE WHO HAD NO FAITH IN THEIR TRUE STRENGTH.
THE ONE WHO FELT SUPERIOR ENOUGH TO PROTECT THEM.
THE ONE WHO WAS ARROGANT!
I AM TO BLAME FOR ALL THAT TRAGEDY!

SO I WILL OVERCOME MY WEAKNESS.

I'LL BELIEVE IN THEM. TRUST THEM.

AND BY LETTING EACH OF THEM DISPLAY THEIR FULLEST POTENTIAL...

...I WILL TAKE BACK MY AMAKUSA-STYLE CROSSIST CHURCH!!

SHE'S REGAINED HER CON-FIDENCE.

HOW-EVER...
VA (VOOM)
GROUNDLESS HOPE IS NAUGHT BUT DELUSION!

HRM...
BASHUN (BSHHHH)
...WHAT IS A SAINT?
ONE BORN WITH PHYSICAL TRAITS SIMILAR TO THE SON OF GOD, WHO IS THUS PERMITTED TO RECEIVE A FRACTION OF HIS STRENGTH.

BUT EVEN THEY COULDN'T POSSIBLY WIELD THE POWER YOU DO.
YOU ARE CLEARLY STRONGER THAN A MERE SAINT.
WHY?

THE ANSWER IS SIMPLE—

THE ADORATION OF MARY.

YOU RESEMBLED MORE THAN JUST THE SON OF GOD, DIDN'T YOU?

YOU RESEMBLED THE HOLY MOTHER AS WELL, AND OBTAINED HER STRENGTH IN THE SAME WAY.

THE MOTHER AND THE SON.
YOU POSSESS TWO CONFLICTING ASPECTS, AND BY SUPERIMPOSING THEM, YOU FORCED THEM INTO A STABLE STATE!
AM I COR-RECT?
...AND WHAT IF YOU ARE?
GOKAN (GRRKKK)
GA GA GA GA GA (WHAM)

DODOOO
(BOOOM)
ドドドオオ

...THAT MEANS YOU HAVE A WEAKNESS.
YOU MUST BE MORE VULNERABLE TO ANTI-SAINT SPELLS THAN ANY OTHER SAINT IN THE WORLD.
...BE-CAUSE IF SO...
IN OTHER WORDS ...

...OUR SAINT-BREAKER!!

...IS THAT WHY ACQUA USED SORCERY FOR DEFENSE, AFTER EASILY HANDLING EVERYTHING ELSE WE THREW AT HIM...!?

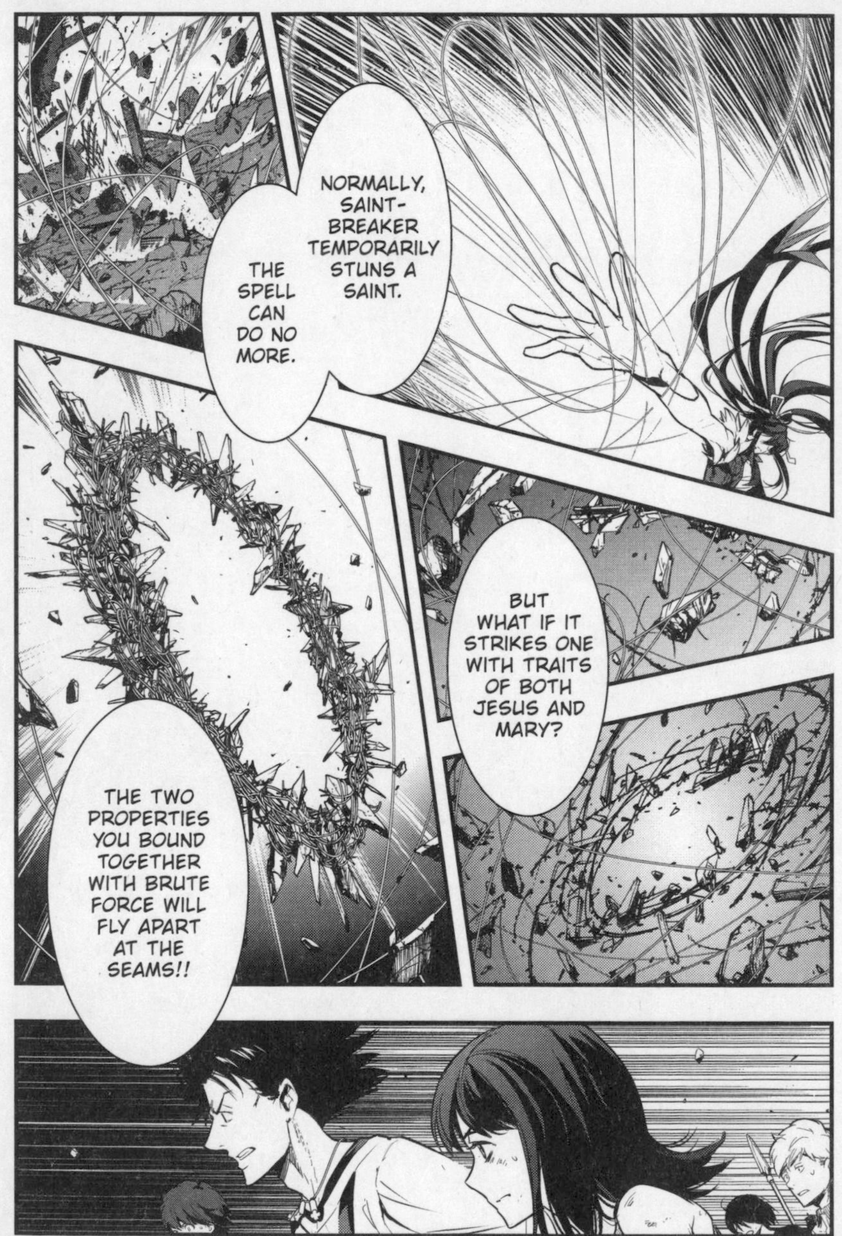
NORMALLY, SAINT-BREAKER TEMPORARILY STUNS A SAINT.
THE SPELL CAN DO NO MORE.
BUT WHAT IF IT STRIKES ONE WITH TRAITS OF BOTH JESUS AND MARY?
THE TWO PROPERTIES YOU BOUND TOGETHER WITH BRUTE FORCE WILL FLY APART AT THE SEAMS!!

DO
DO
DO
DO (RUMBLE)
......
I SEE.

ZA
ZA
ZA
ZA (WSH)
SYMBOLS OF THE CRUCI-FIXION!
SO THAT'S YOUR GAME...!
YOU'RE FALTERING.
LONGINUS!
GRANT US THE FINAL KEY TO THE CRUCI-FIXION!
ZA

ZOKU (CHILL)
...FASCI-NATING.
THE AMAKUSA-STYLE CROSSIST CHURCH, WAS IT?
YOUR NAME IS WORTHY OF REMEM-BERING!
DON (BOOM)

THMMSP
(THE HOLY MOTHER MITIGATES
SEVERE PUNISHMENT.)
TPWATADTGL
(THIS POWER, WHICH AT TIMES APPEALS DIRECTLY TO GOD'S LAW—)
LIWYIMAATH
(LET IT WRAP YOU IN MERCY AND ASCEND TO HEAVEN!)
!!
OH NO!

ANOTHER ONE OF THOSE, AND EVERYONE HERE IS DEAD!

ZUN (SHOOM)
GAH...
AGGGH!

ZAA (SHHH)

!

WHAT... HAP-PENED ...?

IT'S... *DISAP-PEARING* ...?

HIS SPELL ...

HIS SOR-CERY...

DO
(RUMBLE)
DO
DO
DO

IMAGINE...
...BREAKER...!
GURA (STAGGER)

BASTARDS!!!

AHH...
WHOOOOOOAH!!!

BO (BOOM)
ボッ

A Certain Magical Index

A Certain Magical Index

#163 A GUIDE TO FURTHER DISTURBANCE

(WHUMP)
THAT WAS FOR LYING TO ME AND HOGGING ALL THE GOOD PARTS FOR YOURSELF.
......

I'M NOT DONE.

I HAVEN'T PUNCHED YOU FOR LEAVING ENGLAND YET.

BOKI (KRAAAK)

SO LET ME MAKE SURE.

I DON'T WANT TO BE WRONG ABOUT THIS.

DO YOU REALLY PLAN ON LEAVING?

YES. I DO.

GON (WHUMP)
YOU'RE MADE TO BE MORE THAN JUST A MERCENARY.
I'VE BEEN BENDING OVER BACK-WARD TRYING TO GET YOU ACCEPTED AS A FULL-FLEDGED KNIGHT...
...AND YOU'RE JUST KICKING MY EFFORTS TO THE WAYSIDE.

WHAT HAS YOU SO INCENSED ANYWAY?

OR WHAT, ARE YOU TRYING TO BE AN ARTIST OR SOMETHING!?
YOU'VE GOT TO BE INSANE TO CHOOSE A LIFE NOBODY WILL APPRECIATE UNTIL CENTURIES AFTER YOUR DEATH!
I KNOW NOTHING OF ART.
THEN WHAT IS YOUR GOAL, PRAY TELL?
IT'S NOT AS THOUGH I WISH TO DO ANYTHING SPECIAL.

THE KNIGHTS
THE ROYALS
THE PURITANS
OF ENGLAND'S THREE FACTIONS, THE ROYALS ARE EASILY INFLUENCED BY THE PURITANS.
WITH THE ROMAN ORTHODOX CHURCH'S DISQUIETING ACTIONS ABROAD, IT SEEMS SAFE TO ASSUME SOMETHING HAS HAPPENED.
THIS INCIDENT SERVED AS A GOOD EXAMPLE.
......
NO POINT ARGUING ANY FURTHER, THEN.

A FAREWELL GIFT.
THEY'RE PRETTY CONFIDENT IN THIS YEAR'S BATCH.
...IT WOULD BE A WASTE TO DRINK THIS ALONE.
THEN FIND SOME GOOD COMRADES ON YOUR TRAVELS.
GOOD ENOUGH TO WARRANT A GLASS OF IT!
ZA (SHH)
ZA

ONE MORE THING.
THERE SHOULD BE A COMMISSION FOR AN ESCUTCHEON FROM A CRAFTSMAN IN THE LONDON SUBURBS.
DO ME A FAVOR AND CANCEL IT.
IF IT WAS TO REMAIN, I FEEL LIKE REGRETS WOULD TOO.
...I'D NEVER GET RID OF IT.

...I COULD NEVER GET RID OF THAT, DAMN IT...

AHH ...

BACK IN THE USUAL HOSPITAL, HUH?

ARE YOU AWAKE?

HOW DO YOU FEEL?
DOES IT HURT ANYWHERE?

...UHH.
THERE'S NO PAIN, BUT...

...I FEEL KINDA... WORN OUT...
LIKE I HAVE NO ENERGY.
THAT'S TO BE EXPECTED.

AFTER ALL, YOU SNUCK OUT OF YOUR PREVIOUS HOSPITAL STAY—WHEN YOU WERE STRICTLY CONFINED TO BED—AND LAUNCHED A SURPRISE ATTACK ON ACQUA.

YEAH, ABOUT THAT.
I BASICALLY DON'T REMEMBER ANYTHING AFTER SNEAKING OUT...

I SORTA FEEL LIKE I MAY HAVE RUN INTO MISAKA ON THE WAY THERE.
DID I JUST DREAM IT...?

WAIT, THAT'S CRAZY.
HE WAS BOTH A SAINT AND PART OF GOD'S RIGHT SEAT, YEAH? AND YOU BEAT HIM?
DOES THAT MEAN I GOT TO SEE A HISTORIC MOMENT?

Y-YOU WERE THE ONE WHO DID THE MOST, YOU KNOW!?

A SAINT WAS DEFEATED! THERE ARE FEWER THAN TWENTY OF THEM IN THE WHOLE WORLD!
THAT BY ITSELF IS A MIRACLE ...
...BUT ON TOP OF THAT, NOBODY ON OUR SIDE DIED! IT'S LIKE SANTA CLAUS TRIPPED AND SENT HIS PRESENTS SPILLING ALL OVER US!

SO BASICALLY, YOU AND AMAKUSA ARE AMAZING FOR BEATING ACQUA?

UM, NO...
I WASN'T... THAT'S NOT FOR ME TO SAY...

COME TO THINK OF IT, WHAT TIME IS IT?
HOW LONG HAVE I BEEN SLEEPING...?

WAIT, SHIT! WHAT DAY IS IT!?
AREN'T I GONNA RUN OUT OF AB-SENCES SOON!?

AH! N-NO, YOU MUSTN'T GET UP!

......
UM...

....
....
....
I GUESS YOU'RE BACK TO NORMAL, TOUMA.

EEP!
INDEX-SAN!?

I WAS THE ONE SITTING THERE UNTIL A MINUTE AGO...

I TAKE MY EYES OFF YOU FOR ONE SECOND, AND YOU'RE ALREADY DOING THIS!!
YOU HAVEN'T EVEN SAID SORRY FOR SNEAKING OUT OF THE HOSPITAL LIKE THAT!!!

WAIT! THAT'S RIGHT!
I AGREE COM-PLETELY!

I CAN'T BELIEVE YOU'D TRY TO FIGHT ACQUA IN THE STATE YOU WERE IN!
HUH ...?
ACQUA?

ACQUA!? YOU MEAN GOD'S RIGHT SEAT!?
わあ
WAA (CLAMOR)
わあ
WAA
WHY DON'T YOU EVER ASK ME FOR HELP WITH ENEMIES THAT STRONG!?
TOUMAAAA!!

...WHAT SHOULD I DO?

ITSUWA SEEMS TO BE IN THERE, AS WELL AS THAT CHILD...

NEE-CHIIIN?

BA (WHIP)
SUN'S GONNA GO DOWN IF YOU DON'T MAKE A MOVE.

YOU'RE HEADED BACK TO LONDON TOMORROW, RIGHT?
YOU'VE BEEN BLESSED WITH A CHANCE TO VISIT JAPAN IN YOUR VERY BUSY SCHEDULE, SO NOW'S YOUR CHANCE TO THANK KAMIYAN FOR ALL HE'S DONE FOR YOU, NYA.

I AM QUITE AWARE!
HOW TO PUT THIS...
BUT, WELL ...
I'D APPRECIATE WAITING JUST A LITTLE BIT LONGER, AND—

YOU DID BRING THE FALLEN ANGEL MAID OUTFIT WITH YOU, RIGHT?
PFFT!

O-O-O-OF COURSE NOT!!
I FIGURED. THAT'S WHY I BROUGHT THIS ALONG.
'SPECIALLY FOR YOU, MY BASHFUL NEE-CHIN.
ZURU (SHHP)
CHECK IT OUT!
THE FURTHER EVOLUTION OF THE EROTIC FALLEN ANGEL MAID COSTUME SET, NYA!!
...AND WHAT ABOUT THIS IS DIFFERENT?
HUH? WHAT DO YOU MEAN?
LOOK, THE CHEST IS MORE OPEN.
AND THE SKIRT IS MORE TRANSLUCENT—
PIRA (FLIP)
AHH, AHH!
GUKI (GRRKKK)
ANYWAY, NEE-CHIN...
WHAT IS YOUR PLAN, EXACTLY?

I HOPE YOU'RE NOT GONNA JUST WALK IN, SMILE, AND SAY, "THANK YOU, TEE-HEE! ♡" AFTER DRAGGING THIS OUT FOR SO LONG!!
EHH!?

DON'T THINK YOU CAN BUILD SO MUCH SUSPENSE AND THEN SIDESTEP THE ENTIRE ISSUE!!!

THEN WHAT DO YOU WANT OF ME!? ALL I CAN DO IS WHOLE-HEARTEDLY—
YOU CAN AT LEAST GIVE HIM A FEW SQUEEZES AND RUBS, DAMN IT!!

? SQUEEZES OF WHAT?

GET OFF YOUR HIGH HORSE!
WHAT ARE THOSE THINGS ATTACHED TO YOUR BODY EVEN FOR, NEE-CHIN?
QUES-TION! I HAVE A QUES-TION!!

THOSE PROOFS OF MAMMAL-HOOD—
YOUR BOOBS!!?

I WANT YOU TO TELL ME WHAT THEY'RE STUCK TO YOU FOR!!!
...THEY'RE NOT FOR SQUEEZING, AT LEAST...
UGH.
NOT QUITE GETTING THROUGH TO YOU...

BUT, NEE-CHIN, TELL ME HONEST-LY...
...ARE YOU REALLY OKAY WITH GOING AT IT SO SLOWLY?
H-HOW DO YOU MEAN?
I MEAN ITSUWA-CHAN.

I'M SAYING IF IT WAS HER, SHE MIGHT JUST BE OKAY WITH BEING AN EROTIC FALLEN ANGEL MAID.

!!? NO, THAT'S... THAT'S NOT POSSI-BLE...!!
NOT FOR HER!

YOU MAY THINK THAT ITSUWA IS TOO MUCH OF A LATE BLOOMER TO MAKE ANY BOLD MOVES...
...BUT SHE CAN STILL MAKE THE ATTEMPT—IT'S JUST THAT HER HAND-TOWEL PLAN ISN'T WORKING OUT.
AND GIVEN HOW THANKFUL SHE IS TO KAMIYAN, I'M PRETTY SURE SHE'D BE FINE DOING A SIMPLE LITTLE FALLEN ANGEL MAID GETUP.
BUT WHAT ABOUT YOU?
URK...
YOU'RE JUST TOO SHY AND EMBARRASSED. EVEN IF YOU SAID YOU FEEL A DEBT TO KAMIYAN, IT WOULD COME OFF SOUNDING LIKE MERE LIP SERVICE, NYA.
MEAN-ING...
...WHEN IT COMES TO WOMAN-HOOD...
...ITSUWA'S GOT YOU BEAT.

SHEESH. PRIDE'S JUST ABOUT THE ONLY THING YOU'VE GOT, SO YOU DON'T KNOW WHAT IT MEANS TO SWALLOW IT.
WOMAN-HOOD...
I'M WORRIED ABOUT AMAKUSA GOING FORWARD.

HOW DO YOU EXPECT TO GUIDE LOST LAMBS LIKE THAT?
WHEN PUSH COMES TO SHOVE, ARE YOU SURE YOU WON'T ABANDON EVERYONE ELSE?
NO, THAT'S...
YOU'RE GOING TOO FAR FOR A STUPID FALLEN ANGEL MAID COSTUME...

OHH? AM I, NOW?
IF YOU THINK IT'S JUST A STUPID FALLEN ANGEL MAID COSTUME, THEN GO ON, NEE-CHIN, SHOW ME. SHOW ME!
...STAY CALM...I MUST BE CALM...

HE'S CLEARLY TRYING TO TRAP ME.
BUT I WON'T FALL FOR IT!

TO BEGIN WITH, ITSUWA AND THAT GIRL ARE IN THE ROOM RIGHT NOW! WITH THE GIRL'S EIDETIC MEMORY, SHE'LL REMEMBER ME IN THAT MAID OUTFIT FOR THE REST OF HER LIFE. IT'LL STAY IN THE BACK OF HER MIND FOREVER, AHHHHHHHH! IT'S TOO FRIGHTENING TO EVEN IMAGINE...I MUST AVOID
AT ALL COSTS!!
COSTS...!!
EVEN IF I WAS TO DON THAT OUTFIT AS PROOF OF MY SINCERITY, IN A ONE-ON-ONE CONTEST— NO, NO, NO, I HAVE NO INTENT TO WEAR IT! THERE MUST BE ANOTHER WAY! A SANER WAY! I JUST CAN'T THINK OF ONE RIGHT NOW, BUT NEXT TIME FOR SU
THOUGH HOW LONG
BE UNTIL NEXT WE M
...I'M NOW INDEBTE
HIM FOR THE LIVES
THE AMAKUSA ME
WOULDN'T IT BE IN
OTHERWIS
BUSU (SIZZLE)
BUSU
UM... HELLO? NEE-CHIN?
DID I MESS WITH HER A LITTLE TOO MUCH?
FUSHU (FWSHHH)
TSUCHI-MIKADO.
Y-YES?

I AM PREPARED.

THE ITEM, IF YOU WOULD.

HIII (WHEEZE)
BAN (SLAM)
BAN
UWAAAAAAAAAAHHHHH!!!
GAKU
NEVER THOUGHT... ANGELS WERE THAT SCARY...
GAKU (QUIVER)

DAMN!!

TOUMA KAMIJOU.
THOUGH THE BOY BEARS A RARE ABILITY, IT SHOULDN'T HAVE BEEN ENOUGH TO DEFEAT ACQUA.
BUT SO MANY PEOPLE NATURALLY CAME TOGETHER TO PROTECT HIM.

HOW IN THE WORLD COULD ACQUA HAVE LOST...?

A FACTION MADE UP OF HIS FRIENDS AND ALLIES...
I CAN'T UNDER-ESTIMATE IT.
YES, THE BOY IS A POWERFUL OPPONENT INDEED.

WELL, THIS WON'T DO.

ACQUA WAS DEFEATED?

IT SEEMS THEY'VE MATURED A BIT.

YOU...

YOU CAME FROM **BACK THERE**, DIDN'T YOU...

...FIAMMA OF THE RIGHT?

A Certain Magical Index

A Certain Magical Index

#164 THE HOLY RIGHT

FIAMMA OF THE RIGHT!!

IF LOOKS COULD KILL...
QUITE A REAC-TION.
THAT RESPONSE JUST WILL NOT DO.

THEY SAY A LEADER'S TRUE WORTH ONLY MAN-IFESTS IN TIMES OF CRISIS.
IT ALMOST LOOKS AS THOUGH YOU AREN'T WORTHY OF THE POPE'S SEAT.

...WHAT ARE YOU PLANNING?

OUR ATTACK ON ACADEMY CITY USING VENTO, TERRA'S CROWD CONTROL ...
...AND NOW EVEN ACQUA'S INCREDIBLE TALENTS...
EVERY ONE OF THEM A FAILURE.

WHAT MORE IS THERE TO DO?
IS THERE ANY PLAN THAT COULD STOP ACADEMY CITY?

FIRST, WE CRUSH BRITAIN.

WHAT?
DO YOU NOT UNDER-STAND?
NOW THAT WE'VE TAKEN IN THE RUSSIAN CATHOLIC CHURCH, WE HAVE NEAR-COMPLETE CONTROL OVER EUROPE—SAVE FOR BRITAIN.
WE CONTACT EACH NATION AND HAVE THEM STARVE BRITAIN OUT.
...I FAIL TO UNDER-STAND.
I DOUBT TAKING BRITAIN WOULD DEAL A FATAL BLOW TO ACADEMY CITY.
ACADEMY CITY ISN'T EVEN WORTH OUR TIME.

!?
YOU KNOW WHAT BRITAIN HAS.
WE MUST OBTAIN IT AT ALL COSTS.
AND TO GET IT, WE'LL NEED TO MOVE LARGE FORCES AROUND THE TABLE.
AND WHAT IS IT...
...THAT THEY HAVE...?

—

THAT'S... ABSURD...

ARE YOU EVEN CROSSIST...?

WHO KNOWS?
WHAT DO YOU THINK?
DAMN IT!!
SWEAR-ING?
YOU REALLY SHOULD REFRAIN.
YOU'RE SUPPOSED TO BE THE POPE, REMEMBER?

VENTO OF THE FRONT, TERRA OF THE LEFT, ACQUA OF THE BACK...
BUT THEY WERE STILL A CROSSIST ORGANIZATION—GOD'S RIGHT SEAT.
THEY EACH MOVED IN ACCORDANCE WITH THEIR OWN WARPED IDEALS AND CREEDS, AND THEIR THINKING WAS ARROGANT OR HERETICAL AT TIMES.
BUT NOT HIM...
SOMETHING IS DIFFERENT ABOUT FIAMMA OF THE RIGHT!
YOU BASTARD...
DID YOU THINK I'D SIT BACK AND LET YOU DO THIS...!?
YOU WANT TO FIGHT?
AGAINST THE LEADER OF GOD'S RIGHT SEAT?
DON'T LOOK DOWN ON ME.
THIS WILL SILENCE YOU FOR A WHILE...
...OR PERHAPS FOR ETERNITY.

ZUN (WHHHHMP)

BE FILLED WITH STRENGTH!

I AM HE WHO KNOWS ITS PROPER MEANING!

MY ONLY WISH IS FOR THAT STRENGTH TO DEFEAT MY ENEMIES!

I DECLARE TO APOSTLES ONE THROUGH TWELVE!

I BEG THE LORD WHO CANNOT BE COUNTED!

SFX: HYUUU (WHISTLE)

THE SYMBOLS OF JESUS AND THE APOSTLES?

KIN (KRRRK)

LIE IDLE THERE FOR ABOUT FORTY YEARS.

HAVE A GOOD, LONG TASTE OF SELF-ISOLATION.
AND USE THIS CHANCE TO REFORM YOUR IMMATURE MIND!

THIS LAND FUNCTIONS AS ONE MASSIVE SOUL ARM TO BOLSTER MY SPELL.

THE POWER I WIELD IN ST. PETER'S BASILICA IS SACRED, AND HAS GUIDED MORE THAN TWO BILLION FAITHFUL OVER TWO THOUSAND YEARS—

A SINGLE ARROGANT MAN WILL NOT BREAK FREE OF IT.

PIKU (TWITCH)

ピク

DON'T BOTHER.

ONLY TWO BILLION PEOPLE?

ONLY TWO THOUSAND YEARS?

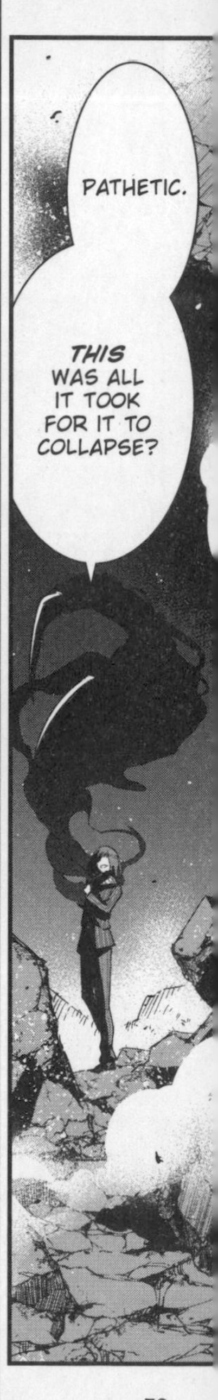
PATHETIC.
THIS WAS ALL IT TOOK FOR IT TO COLLAPSE?

AND MICHAEL, THE ANGEL OF THE RIGHT— HE WHO IS LIKE GOD.

HIS OWN RIGHT HAND POSSESSED INCREDIBLE POWER.

ENOUGH TO SLAY MANY A FALLEN ANGEL AND EVEN CUT DOWN LUCIFER, THE BEARER OF LIGHT.

BUT...

...IT GOES WITHOUT SAYING THAT NO NORMAL HUMAN CAN WIELD SUCH POWER.

WHETHER IT'S SAINTS OR GOD'S RIGHT SEAT, WE'RE ALL STILL FLESH-AND-BLOOD HUMANS.

I'M JUST A REGULAR HUMAN.

DO YOU GET IT, MR. POPE?

UNFOR-TUNATELY.

I'VE GOT THIS WONDERFUL CRYSTALLIZATION OF RIGHT-HANDED MIRACLES, BUT NO OUTPUT TERMINAL FOR EXPRESSING THEM.

AS YOU CAN SEE, I'M ONLY ABLE TO DRAW OUT A TINY BIT OF POWER LIKE THIS.

HEY.

LISTEN.

WOULDN'T YOU WANT THAT?

THE HOLY RIGHT, SYMBOL OF ALL MIRACLES.
THE POWER OF THE RIGHT, WHICH CRUSHED ALL EVILS AND BOUND THE KING OF DEVILS IN THE PIT OF HELL.
THE POWER THAT BROUGHT ABOUT A THOUSAND YEARS OF PEACE.
WHAT IF THERE WAS A ***RIGHT HAND*** THAT COULD DRAW THAT POWER OUT IN ITS ENTIRETY?
YOU... CAN'T MEAN ...
I'D BE ABLE TO WIELD IT.
BUT TO DO SO, I'LL NEED TO PREPARE.

THERE'S SOMETHING I NEED TO RESTRAIN SUCH INCREDIBLE POWER.

AND THAT'S INCREDIBLE KNOWLEDGE—BEYOND THAT OF MANKIND.

THE INDEX OF FORBIDDEN BOOKS—
!

THE BRITISH HAVE PREPARED SOMETHING QUITE NICE, HAVEN'T THEY?

I...
...WON'T LET... YOU...

ISN'T THIS FUN?

...ARE SO ABSURD— BUT OH SO ENJOYABLE.

ONE-SIDED CONTESTS LIKE THESE...

ZU

ZU

ZU

ZU

ZU (SHP)

HMM?

ODD. ALL OF ROME SHOULD BE A PILE OF RUBBLE RIGHT NOW.

YOU TOOK THE FULL BRUNT OF THAT YOURSELF?
YOU'RE SOMETHING ELSE.

HAH!
JUST LOOK AT YOU NOW.
WOUNDS OF HONOR FROM SAVING LOST LAMBS, ARE THEY?
......
BRITAIN ...
GO...TO BRITAIN...
THAT'S WHERE...
...FIAMMA'S TARGET IS.
GOFU (KOFF)
NOBODY GIVES ME ORDERS.

BUT I GUESS I CAN LET IT SLIDE THIS TIME, SINCE WE'RE BOTH TRYING TO KILL THE SAME SHITHEAD.

KEH HEH.

THAT'S SOME GOOD HOSTILITY.

AND YOU'RE IN LUCK.

IF I HAD MY USUAL WEAPON, YOU'D ALL BE DEAD WHERE YOU STAND.

THERE ARE SIGNS OF INTERNAL STRIFE WITHIN THE ROMAN CHURCH.

IT SEEMS THE POPE WAS MIXED UP IN IT AND WOUNDED. THE SITUATION IS UNPREDICTABLE.

FROM THE AMOUNT OF MANA WE OBSERVED, THE VATICAN SHOULD BE MASSIVELY DAMAGED...
...BUT WE HAVEN'T BEEN ABLE TO CONFIRM ANY YET.
HM.
IT'S IN THE MIDST OF THE CITY, ISN'T IT?
THERE WON'T BE MUCH DAMAGE.
ゴロ
GORO (SLUMP)
...YOU DAMNED MARTYR.

I'M SURE YOU WERE SMILING TOO.

DAMNED... MARTYR...

PLAN INFLUENCE COEFFICIENT FOR SPECIMEN "IMAGINE BREAKER": 98%.
STRENGTH AS MAIN PLAN BACKBONE, ALONG WITH ACADEMY CITY NUMBER ONE, OPERATING ACCORDING TO ESTIMATES.
SEVERAL HOURS UNTIL COMPLETE RECOVERY OF THE UNDERLINE.
ILLOGICAL-PHENOMENA-REJECTING "POINT CENTRAL 0" MAINTAINING STABILITY LEVEL 3.
INTEGRATED PROCESSING OF PRE-MALFUNCTION DATA PROGRESSING.

A Certain Magical Index

A Certain Magical Index

LONDON
!
"HOW TO MAKE A LONG-DISTANCE RELATIONSHIP WORK"...?

LET'S SEE...

"THE KEY IS MAKING SURE HE REMEMBERS YOU.

GU (LEAN)

"LEAVE A STRONG IMPRESSION ON HIM AS A WOMAN SO HE DOESN'T FORGET"...?

A STRONG IMPRES-SION...

O-OUR PRIEST-ESS IS ALWAYS A STEP AHEAD!!

WHO KNEW SHE HAD SUCH A TRICK UP HER SLEEVE...

GENIUS
AVERAGE
I TRIED SO HARD TO GET CLOSER TO HIM, BUT SHE STOLE ALL MY EFFORTS IN THE END...
HUGE CHEST, HIDDEN
HUGE CHEST, OBVIOUS EVEN UNDER CLOTHES
MAYBE A SIMPLE SORCERER LIKE ME JUST CAN'T COMPETE WITH A SAINT...

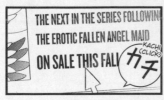

MAX80%OFF
THE NEXT IN THE SERIES FOLLOWIN
THE EROTIC FALLEN ANGEL MAID
ON SALE THIS FALL
カチ
KACHI (CLICK)

TH-THIS IS...

A GREAT FAIRY...
...FLASHY MAID...??

WAAAAHHHH!!!
I...I COULD NEVER WEAR SOMETHING LIKE THIS!!!

THIS IS GETTING TEDIOUS ...
MAYBE WE SHOULD BUY IT AND LEAVE IT IN FRONT OF HER ROOM.
MM. WE'LL NEED TO SHED BLOOD AND SWEAT IF WE WISH TO BEAR WITNESS TO THE BATTLE BETWEEN A FALLEN ANGEL AND A GREAT FAIRY.
WOULD YOU GUYS PUT A SOCK IN IT AND DO YOUR JOB ALREADY?

ZOKU (SHUDDER)

THE IDEAL EVENT WOULD BE THE BALL AT THE QUEEN'S RESIDENCE, WHICH ALSO SERVES AS A BIRTHDAY CELEBRATION FOR A MEMBER OF THE HOUSE OF LORDS.

?

THERE ARE SEVERAL OTHER OPTIONS IN OCTOBER, SUCH AS THE SOIREE AT WINDSOR CASTLE AND THE BOAT PARTY IN LIVERPOOL.
WHILE THE GUESTS AT THE BALL ARE RATHER MORE DINGY, NOBODY THERE WOULD UNTHINKINGLY PESTER A LADY.

LOOKING FURTHER, THERE IS THE EVENT AT BUCKINGHAM PALACE FOR HALLOW-EEN—
EXCUSE ME...
...KNIGHT LEADER?

I'M NOT ACTUALLY LOOKING TO MAKE MY HIGH-SOCIETY DEBUT.

YOU WERE THE ONE WHO ASKED ME TO TEACH YOU HOW TO CARRY YOURSELF IN THE UNITED KINGDOM.

WHEN I HAD JUST ARRIVED IN ENGLAND, YES...

...BUT I'M A MEMBER OF THE CHURCH. IS IT REALLY NECESSARY TO ATTEND BALLS?

LEADING A JUST AND PROPER LIFE AS A DISCIPLE AND POLISHING YOUR BEAUTY AS A LADY ARE TWO DIFFERENT THINGS.

IN FACT, I'D HEARD THAT YOU'D STARTED TO SHOW INTEREST IN THAT WAY OF LIFE...
WHERE ON EARTH DID YOU HEAR THAT?

...HMM. HOW STRANGE.

BFFHGHT!?

WAS THE INTEL ABOUT THE EROTIC FALLEN ANGEL MAID FALSE...?

GOHO (COUGH)

GOHOHO

SUCH BEHAVIOR ILL BEFITS A PROPER LADY.

AND WHILE I CAN COUNTENANCE THE "EROTIC" AND "MAID" PARTS, THE SAME DOES NOT GO FOR THE "FALLEN ANGEL" PORTION.

AS YOU LEARN HOW A NOBLEWOMAN BEHAVES IN HIGH SOCIETY, YOU COULD ALSO INTRODUCE YOURSELF ***AS A WARRIOR.***
YOU COULD MAKE THIS SERVE BOTH YOUR ENDS.
...SO THAT'S WHAT HE'S REALLY AFTER.
I HEARD HE CAME FOR ME WHILE I WAS AWAY, FLOWERS IN HAND, TO INVITE ME TO A BALL...

KNIGHT LEADER.
I'VE NO INTENTION OF TRANSFERRING FROM THE PURITANS TO THE KNIGHTS.
MY SWORDSMANSHIP IS BUT A SINGLE PART OF MY TECHNIQUES—AND MY FAITH IS AT ITS CORE.
I DO NOT WALK THE PATH OF A TRUE SWORDSWOMAN.
HMM.

IN ANY CASE, I NEED TO DEAL WITH THIS PROBLEM...
HOW IS THE EUROTUNNEL LOOKING?
NO HOPE FOR RESTORATION.
I'VE HEARD TENSIONS WITH FRANCE ARE ON THE RISE.
WE'RE STILL INVESTIGATING THE CAUSE...
...BUT APPARENTLY, EVEN PARLIAMENT IS STRUGGLING TO PLACATE THE MILITARY'S CALLS FOR A PREEMPTIVE STRIKE ON THEM.

SEVERAL GROUPS WITHIN OUR BORDERS ARE TAKING ADVANTAGE OF THE CONFUSION AS WELL.

SOME ARE ANTI-GOVERNMENTAL, AND WE SHOULD ASSUME SOME OF THOSE ARE SORCERER'S SOCIETIES.

ENEMIES WITHIN AND WITHOUT.
WE BOTH HAVE FULL PLATES, IT SEEMS.

INDEED.

THERE WON'T BE ANY TIME FOR IDLENESS.

AND THAT INCLUDES WORRYING OVER WHAT COLOR DRESS TO WEAR TO A BALL!

#165 DIRECT FLIGHT TO THE LAND OF SORCERY

HOW'S THIS ICHI-HANARAN FESTI-VAL...
...GONNA BE ANY DIFFERENT FROM BACK IN MIDDLE SCHOOL?
IF WE GOT A BIGGER BUDGET, WE'D BE ABLE TO DO MORE.
NYA. THE ONLY ONES GIVING OUT FUNDING ARE THE COMPETITIVE SCHOOLS SERIOUS ABOUT THE OPEN CAMPUS.

MEANWHILE, AVERAGE SCHOOLS LIKE OURS MIGHT AS WELL BE IN A DIFFERENT WORLD...

Executive
mmittee
THAT MEANS MY TIME HAS COME AT LAST!

THE WORLD'S BIGGEST CULTURE FESTIVAL IS AROUND THE CORNER, AND YOU THREE ARE GOING TO BE HELPING.
I MEAN, WON'T WE JUST BE RUNNING A STALL OR SOMETHING? AND THEN IT'LL BE OVER.

IT WILL ***NOT*** BE OVER! TRY USING YOUR TIME A LITTLE MORE EFFECTIVELY, WHY DON'T YOU?
YOU MIGHT FIND A WHOLE NEW PART OF YOURSELF YOU NEVER KNEW ABOUT.
ESPECIALLY YOU, YOU SPIKY-HAIRED JERK. I SEE YOU PLAYING WITH ROLLED-UP ERASER PIECES!!
OH, COME ON. I DON'T NEED ANY NEW PARTS OF ME.
I MEAN, THE MOST THAT COULD HAPPEN WOULD BE LIKE... THINKING I'M SUPER INTO MAIDS, BUT FINDING OUT I ACTUALLY PREFER WAITRESSES.

NYAAAA!! THAT'S EXTREMELY IMPORTANT!!
MAIDS CAN DO A WAITRESS'S JOB, BUT WAITRESSES CAN'T DO A MAID'S WORK! HOW CAN YOU EVEN FORGET SOMETHING LIKE THAT!?
WAI
WAI (CHATTER)
GYAI (BLATHER)
HEH ...
THE TWO OF YA ARE IDIOTS. THERE'S NO LAW SAYIN' YOU CAN'T LIKE 'EM BOTH.

SHUT UP!
GO (SLAM)

AAAAH!
GORO (TUMBLE)
GORO
GO

OWW...

......
ing looked over
in class you need
character traits.
A l some kind
of pecial skill for
work

...HEY.
HIMEGAMI?
IF SOMETHING'S BOTHERING YOU, YOU KNOW YOU CAN TALK TO ME.
IT'S FINE.

I WANT TO DO THIS MYSELF.
OH. UM, OKAY.

...IF I COULD JUST GIVE ONE PIECE OF ADVICE...

...DIDN'T YOU ALREADY HAVE A NICE AND PEACEFUL CHARACTER TRAIT? YOUR COOKING SKILLS ARE FLAWLESS.
...!

YOU DO MAKE YOUR OWN LUNCH TO BRING TO SCHOOL EVERY DAY, AFTER ALL!
HA HA HA...
I'M A FAN OF COOKING FOR MYSELF TOO, BUT I'M NOWHERE NEAR AS GOOD AS ALL THAT.

OKAAAY! HOME-ROOM IS START-ING!

ADULT WOMAN (LOOKS TWELVE)

135 CM

WIDE-SPANNING KNOWLEDGE OF MANY FIELDS, INCLUDING PYROKINESIS (HER SPECIALIZATION)

CAN'T RESIST BEER OR CIGARETTES

IT'S TOO MUCH!

PAAAAA (SHIIIINE)

GAKUU (SLUMP)
... HNG...

H-HIMEGAMI!?
... NOPE.
I CAN'T DO IT.
THERE'S NO WAY TO STAND OUT AMONG WALKING BUNDLES OF CHARACTER TRAITS LIKE THAT.
I CAN'T
HEEEEY!
GET AHOLD OF YOURSELF!

...HAAH.
I'D RATHER PEOPLE NOT VIEW MY ROTTEN LUCK AS A CHARACTER TRAIT.

HEY, THAT'S...

POKEEE
ポケー

HAAAA-AHHH...

I CAN HELP YOU TOO!!

I...
I REALLY WENT AND STEPPED IN IT WITH THAT...

JUST THINKING BACK ON IT MAKES MY SIDES ITCH LIKE HELL.

WHAT HAS YOU IN SUCH A TIZZY, ONEE-SAMA?

UWAAAAAHHHH!

OHH, THIS IS BAD...

HOW AM I SUPPOSED TO FACE HIM NOW?

IT IS YOU! BIRI BIRI!

WHAT ARE YOU DOING HERE?
BIYA (FLINCH)

NO...
I...
NOTH...

...NOTHING IMPORTANT! IT DOESN'T MATTER!
I WAS JUST KICKING THIS VENDING MACHINE, AS USUAL!!

THAT, UH, DOES KINDA MATTER. YOU SHOULD REALLY STOP THAT.

UM.
SO, YOU...
YOU'RE ALL HEALED UP NOW?

YEAH, PRETTY MUCH.
THEN... OH.
MY MIND WAS SO HAZY I HARDLY REMEMBER ANYTHING, BUT...
I'D REALLY APPRECIATE YOU NOT TELLING ANYONE ELSE.
...I GUESS THAT MEANS YOU FOUND OUT, DIDN'T YOU?
PEOPLE WOULD GET WEIRD AROUND ME IF THEY KNEW I HAD AMNESIA...
IT'D BE GREAT IF YOU COULD JUST ACT THE WAY YOU ALWAYS DO WITH ME.
O-OH...
....
....
I FIGURED IT'D BE AWKWARD THE NEXT TIME I MET HIM, BUT...

...I'M RELIEVED...

...THAT I CAN TALK TO HIM AGAIN.

ALSO, VENDING MACHINES ASIDE, YOU REALLY SHOULDN'T DO HIGH KICKS IN A SKIRT.

JUST 'COS YOU'RE WEARING SHORT PANTS DOESN'T CHANGE THE FACT THAT PEOPLE CAN SEE YOUR ENTIRE THIGHS, YOU KNOW?

DON'T BE A PERV!
BA (WHP)

UGH...
RIGHT.

!?

LEMON
COFF
PI
(BEEP)
ピ
GASHAN
(KLUNK)
ガシャン

WHAT'S UP WITH YOU?

MISAKA, OF ALL PEOPLE, PUTTING COINS IN TO BUY A DRINK LIKE A NORMAL PERSON?

YOU'RE BEING WEIRDLY MEEK TODAY.

PASHI
(BZZZT)

EEEEP...
DON'T "EEP" ME!!!
BACHI (CRACKLE)
BACHI
BACHI

SO THEY RESCUED ALL 370 PEOPLE FROM THAT UNDER-WATER TUNNEL?

GOTTA HAND IT TO THE BRITISH DIVERS.

PERSIMMON SEEDS

10% MORE

TOUMA?

WHAT HAPPENED TO THE TIPS OF YOUR HAIR?

HUH...?

...JUST GOT CAUGHT IN A LITTLE ACCIDENTAL EXPLOSION.

BUCHI (YOINK) ブチ

THIS KOTATSU THING IS SO WARM AND COZY...

...ANY-WAY...

RIGHT?

NOW DO YOU UNDERSTAND THE WONDERS OF JAPANESE HEATING TECHNOLOGY, INDEX!?

MUNYA (MMMN) ムニャ

ムニャ MUNYA

GOROGORO (LAAAAZE) ゴロゴロ

OH, BUT THERE'S A TRAP! IF YOU FALL ASLEEP IN ONE, YOU'LL CATCH A COLD, SO BE CAREFUL.

...SO I SAY...
...BUT MAN, A KOTATSU IS AN IRRESISTIBLE THING...
MAYBE WE SHOULD JUST LAZE AROUND UNTIL IT'S TIME FOR BED...

FGHUNH?
BI PI BI PI BI PI BI PI
(BLEEP)

HELLO?

Kami-yan!

You doin' all right?

WHAT DO YOU WANT, TSUCHIMIKADO? WILL THIS TAKE LONG?

Well, yeah.

Where should I start...

I guess I'll just cut to the chase for now.

You're going to Britain—like, now.

ooooooooooooooooooooooooo
ooooooooooooooooooooooooo
ooooooooooooooooooooooooo

HUH !?
We've already got a plane for you.

HUH? HEY, WAIT!
BRITAIN !?
NOTHING GOOD EVER HAPPENS WHEN I TRAVEL OVERSEAS!

AND THAT'S WHERE THE ENGLISH PURITAN CHURCH HQ IS! THAT'S EXTRA BAD!!
I know how you feel, Kamiyan.
But it's too late.

GASHAN (CRASH)
ガシャン
GORON (ROLL)
ゴロン
BUSHUUU (BSHHHHHH)
ブシュ
UGH...

GABA (BOLT)
がばっ
Z

WHERE ARE WE!?
HEY! INDEX!!

GO (RUMBLE)
GO
GO
GO
GO
IT'S EXACTLY THE SAME AS LAST TIME!
TSUCHIMIKA-DOOOOOOOO!!
YAAAWN...
TOUMA... I'M HUNGRY.

A Certain Magical Index

EUROPE SURE IS A MESS.
THAT'S RIGHT.
JUST AS YOU SAID.
THE ROME-RUSSIA FACTION IS BACKING FRANCE.
IN RESPONSE, THE U.K. SEEMS TO BE SEEKING HELP FROM NOT ONLY ACADEMY CITY, BUT THE AMERICANS AS WELL.
THIS WON'T END AT AN EVERYDAY WAR BETWEEN TWO NATIONS.
LOOKS LIKE THAT BASTARD FIAMMA IS FINE WITH REDUCING ALL OF EUROPE TO A SEA OF FLAMES TO ACHIEVE HIS GOALS...
AND THE MOST AGGRAVATING PART IS THAT HE'S THE ONE WITH CONTROL OVER THE ROME-RUSSIA FACTION.
NOBODY IS LEFT TO FOLLOW ANY ORDERS YOU OR I MIGHT GIVE.
WE DON'T HAVE THE AUTHORITY.
WILL YOU GO ANYWAY?

SURE, I SUPPOSE YOU BRING A LOT OF BRAWN TO THE TABLE.

IF WE WERE JUST SLUGGING IT OUT, YOU'D PROBABLY BEAT ME.

BUT WHEN IT'S THE NATION ITSELF...

...OR THE WORLD ITSELF...

...THAT'S ABOUT TO BE DESTROYED IN A CALAMITY, HOW FAR WILL THAT STRENGTH REALLY TAKE YOU?

WHAT-EVER.

IF YOU WANT TO GO, IT DOESN'T MATTER TO ME.

I DON'T HAVE THE AUTHORITY TO STOP YOU, AND I DON'T HAVE ANY DUTY TO CONCERN MYSELF WITH YOUR LIFE EITHER.
BUT I WILL TELL YOU MY PLAN.
I'M NOT GOING.

EH?
DON'T TALK DOWN TO ME.
YOU'RE SAYING I'M SCARED?
I CAN'T EXACTLY USE MY DIVINE JUDGMENT SPELL ANY-MORE, YOU KNOW.
GOD'S RIGHT SEAT CAN'T USE NORMAL SPELLS OR SOUL ARMS—WELL, YOU ASIDE, I GUESS.
I'LL BE HOPPING FROM PLACE TO PLACE, GETTING EVERYTHING I NEED READY.
BECAUSE I THINK I'VE GOT A BEAD ON SOMETHING THAT'LL REALLY MAKE FIAMMA SQUIRM.
NOBODY GIVES ME ORDERS.
YOU WALK YOUR PATH, AND I'LL WALK MINE.

#166 SKYBUS 365 ①

BEEF OR FISH!

BEEF OR FISH!

BEEF!!

OR...

...FIIISH!!!

YOU'RE EXCITED FOR THE IN-FLIGHT MEAL. I GET IT!

ALL RIGHT, ALL RIGHT.

LONDON

ANYWAY, I CAN'T BELIEVE WE'RE SUDDENLY GOING TO THE U.K.

I APPRE-CIATE HIM GETTING ALL OUR LUGGAGE READY...
...BUT YOU'RE SUPPOSED TO GET PERMISSION IN ADVANCE TO LEAVE ACADEMY CITY, AND HE JUST SNUCK US OUT.
THE CHEAT...

WE'LL ARRIVE IN EDINBURGH TOMORROW AFTER-NOON...
...AND THEN WE HAVE TO GET ON ANOTHER FLIGHT TO LONDON. HOW EXHAUSTING.
WILL IT REALLY TAKE THAT LONG?
WE HAD TO SQUEEZE THROUGH THE WAIT-LIST FOR THIS.
THE ONE THEY ORIGINALLY RESERVED WAS A DIRECT FLIGHT. IT WOULD HAVE GOTTEN US TO LONDON IN TWO HOURS...
...BUT WOULD YOU HAVE RATHER GOTTEN ON THAT PLANE AGAIN?
...I THINK I LIKE PLANES WHERE YOUR FOOD DOESN'T FLY AWAY BETTER.

WELL, SPHINX SHOULD BE GETTING TO LONDON ABOUT NOW, AT LEAST.
FORGIVE ME...
MEEGYA-AHHH!!
(TRAITORS!!)
I HOPE SPHINX ISN'T LOST ON HIS OWN.
AMAKUSA'S PICKING HIM UP. HE'LL BE FINE.
THEY KNOW WHAT THEY'RE DOING WHEN IT COMES TO THIS STUFF.

BUT, TOUMA...

...WHY DO WE HAVE TO GO TO ENGLAND ANYWAY?

UHH... RIGHT.

LET'S SEE...

SEEMS LIKE... SOME BIG SORCERY-RELATED TROUBLE HAPPENED OVER THERE, SO THEY WANTED TO SUMMON YOU THERE AS AN OFFICIAL STATE THING...

AND, UH... THEY WANTED ME TO COME, SINCE I'M CUR-RENTLY YOUR GUARDIAN.
YOU, MY GUARDIAN? THAT'S KIND OF ANNOYING.
KIDS WHO GET OTHERS TO MAKE FOOD FOR THEM EVERY DAY DON'T GET TO TALK.
...BUT THIS MEANS ...

...WE'RE GOING BACK TO YOUR HOMELAND.

RIGHT, INDEX?

YEAH.

BUT IT DOESN'T FEEL REAL.

I MEAN, I DON'T REMEMBER ANYTHING BEFORE A YEAR AGO.

......
NO MEMORIES, HUH...

TOUMA...

WHEN DOES THE AIRPLANE FOOD GET HERE?

IT'S NIGHT-TIME. IT'S PROBABLY GONNA BE LIKE NINE MORE HOURS.
M... M...!?!!!!??
WE TOOK OFF PRETTY LATE IN THE DAY, AFTER ALL.

BUT IF I HAVE TO WAIT THAT LONG, I'LL WITHER UP AND DIE...
L-LOOK, DRINKS ARE FREE! HAVE SOME WATER, GO TO SLEEP, AND IT'LL BE BREAKFAST BEFORE YOU KNOW IT!

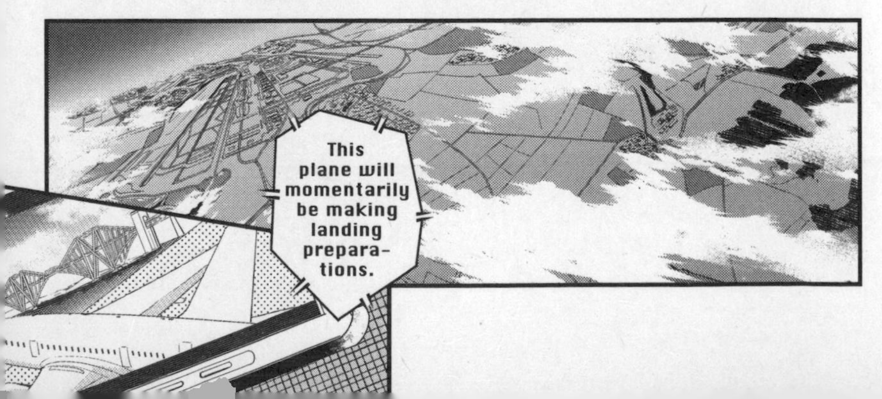
This plane will momentarily be making landing preparations.

THEY'VE GOT A ROW OF CONTAINERS DOWN THERE.

HMMM!

THAT MAN IN WORK CLOTHES—
HE'S EATING A SANDWICH!!!

NO FAIR! I WANT A SANDWICH TOO!!
WATABATA (FLAIL)
CALM DOWN! THE SANDWICH ISN'T GONNA WARP INTO YOUR HANDS BY CLIMBING ALL OVER ME!
GAKON (CLUNK)

...?

SA (SHF)

IS SOMETHING THE MATTER, SIR?

I'M TERRIBLY SORRY FOR THE WAIT.
THE EUROTUNNEL IS CLOSED BECAUSE OF AN ACCIDENT, SO WE WILL TEMPORARILY BE ASSISTING IN FERRYING CARGO ACROSS THE CHANNEL.
WE'RE TAKING EVERY MEASURE TO ENSURE IT'S AS LITTLE OF A DISRUPTION TO YOUR SCHEDULES AS POSSIBLE...

HAAH... IS THE U.K. REALLY IN THAT BAD A SHAPE?
THEY'RE MANAGING BY SEA AND AIR FOR NOW...
THIS FLIGHT IS SLATED TO TRANSPORT EMERGENCY GOODS, LIKE MEDICINE, LIQUID FOOD, AND FRESH FOOD-STUFFS.

...FLIGHT...
FOOD...
IN-FLIGHT MEAL ...
BEEF...

THERE WAS THAT EXPLO-SION IN THE UNDER-WATER TUNNEL...
...AND THEY COULDN'T RULE OUT TERROR-ISM.
THIS BETTER NOT BE LINKED TO ENGLAND CALLING INDEX BACK...

BEEF OR FISH!!!
WHOA!
BEEF OR FIIIISH!!
CALM YOURSELF!! YOU HAVE TO PICK JUST ONE!
GABU (CHOMP)
GYAAAH! MY HEAD IS NOT BEEF OR FISH!
GAJI (GNAW)
KAJI (CHEW)
GAJIGA
I-I'LL BRING SOME RIGHT AWAY!!
......
WHAT'S GOING ON HERE?

THOSE SEATS SHOULD HAVE BEEN EMPTY...

...SHE'S TAKING A WHILE...
GURURURURU (GROWWWWWL)

I'M GETTING HUNGRY MYSELF. I'M GONNA GO CHECK.
!!
I'LL COME TOO!!
YOU'LL JUST BOTHER THEM. WAIT HERE.

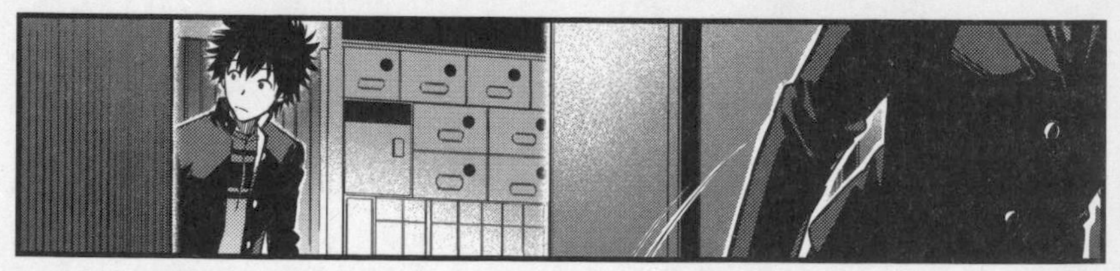

SA
(SWF)
'SCUSE ME...

SHE SEEMS BUSY...
DID I GET IN HER WAY?

HUH...? THE DOOR'S OPEN.

BLOOD ...!?
SU (SLIDE)
WH- WHAT HAP- PENED?
SAW IT, DID YOU?

DAN (SLAM)
GAHAH!!
CAPTAIN. WE HAVE A PROB-LEM.
A PASSENGER SPOTTED THE BLOODSTAINS BEFORE I COULD CLEAN THEM.
HOW SHOULD I PROCEED?

A Certain Magical Index

#167 SKYBUS 365 ②

WHAT? TERRORISTS !?

YES.
AIR TRAFFIC CONTROL SAYS THEY'VE INFILTRATED THE PLANE.
SHH.

THEY SAY IF WE DON'T MEET THEIR DEMANDS, THIS PLANE WILL GO DOWN IN FLAMES.
YOU'RE KID-DING...

THE BLOOD-STAINS WERE FROM MY COLLEAGUE.
SHE WAS AMBUSHED FROM BEHIND.
HER LIFE ISN'T IN DANGER, BUT SHE'S STILL UN-CONSCIOUS.

WAIT, HANG ON.

YOU DON'T SUSPECT ME IN ALL THIS, DO YOU!?
NO, OF COURSE NOT.

...THE TERRORISTS ARE DEMANDING THE DESTRUC-TION OF THE MASTER RECORDER FOR THE FOUR LARGEST AIRLINES.
CAP-TAIN...
THEIR ULTIMATE GOAL MUST BE TO COMPLETELY CUT OFF THE U.K.'S AIR ROUTES.

I'M ONLY TELLING YOU THIS BECAUSE YOU SAW PART OF IT.
WE CAN'T HAVE YOU SPREADING WORD OF WHAT'S GOING ON TO THE OTHER PASSEN-GERS.
THEY COULD PANIC.

APOLOGIES, BUT YOU'LL HAVE TO STAY HERE UNTIL THINGS SETTLE DOWN.
W-WAIT A SECOND!

WE NEED AS MANY PEOPLE AS WE CAN GET!

IF THERE'RE TERRORISTS ON BOARD, WE DON'T HAVE TIME FOR THIS!

I CAN HELP Y—

AN AMATEUR RUNNING AROUND AS HE PLEASES COULD RUIN EVERYTHING.

CAN YOU TAKE RESPONSIBILITY FOR THE FIVE HUNDRED SOULS ON BOARD THIS PLANE?
...!

THEN KEEP QUIET.
IF YOU'RE NOT HAPPY, FEEL FREE TO SUE ME AFTER ALL THIS.
I'M SORRY. PLEASE BE PATIENT.
ガシャン
GASHAN (KACHAK)

BEEP

ERROR

DAMN!
THE HATCH NEEDS MORE THAN A FLIGHT ATTENDANT'S SECURITY PRIVILEGES TO OPEN...

BUT THE THING IN THE HOLD IS MY LAST RESORT...
IF THOSE SEATS HAD BEEN EMPTY LIKE THEY WERE SUP-POSED TO BE, THIS WOULD HAVE GONE A LOT MORE SMOOTHLY!!

...!

HOW FAR DID HE GO...?
TOUMA?

KACHI (CHK)
KACHI

...DAMN!

DAMN, DAMN, DAMN!!!

OF ALL THE TIMES FOR THE CONNECTOR TO BREAK! NOW I CAN'T INJECT THE PROGRAM TO INTERFERE WITH THE EMERGENCY-LANDING SAFETY MECHANISM...!

THAT'S TOUMA'S SEAT.

MISTER?
SAFETY MECHA-NISM...?
WHAT ARE YOU DOING?
JUST 120 SECONDS ...
WHY COULDN'T YOU WAIT 120 DAMN SECONDS?

THIS KNIFE IS MADE OF ANIMAL BONES.

METAL DETECTORS CAN'T CATCH IT.

ONE MOVE, AND YOU'RE DEAD.

GET UP.

UGH...

I WONDER IF INDEX IS OKAY ON HER OWN.
HOPE SHE'S NOT GOING NUTS FROM HUNGER.
THAT'D CAUSE AN EVEN BIGGER PANIC...
BATAN (KACHAK)

Va vite dans ta chambre!
<Get in! Now!>

BATABATA (STRUGGLING)

EEK ...!

DO
(BAM)
DO
BAN
(SLAM)

Gah... hah!

YOU...
...SON OF A BITCH!!!...
URGH!
DODO (THUD)

GOJAAA
(KRRRNCHHHH)

INDEX! ARE YOU ALL RIGHT!?

THE EMERGENCY-LANDING SAFETY...?

YEAH.
INDEX SAW IT WHILE THAT GUY WAS DOING SOMETHING IN MY SEAT.
GACHA (KACHAK)
ガチャッ

SO THEN THE TERRORIST WAS...
TRYING TO TAKE CONTROL OF IT TO THREATEN US, MOST LIKELY.
ALL RIGHT, I UNDERSTAND WHAT'S GOING ON.

...THE SKYBUS 365 IS DESIGNED SO THAT SENSORS WILL DETECT THE IMPACT FROM A BELLY LANDING AND AUTOMATICALLY STOP ALL THE ENGINES.

I APOLOGIZE FOR GETTING YOU TWO WRAPPED UP IN THIS.
IT WAS MY FAILING.
BUT THANKFULLY, WE'VE SECURED THE CULPRIT BEFORE THINGS ESCALATED.

IS THAT... REALLY IT?
ATTACKING A FLIGHT ATTENDANT? TRYING TO KILL INDEX? SEEMS PRETTY AD HOC FOR A CRIMINAL.
SOMETHING ABOUT THIS ISN'T RIGHT...

I'LL CONTACT AIR TRAFFIC CONTROL IMMEDIATELY.
......

...? WHAT!?
EXPLAIN THE SITUATION! DID THE TERRORIST DO THAT TOO!?

I-I DON'T KNOW!!
WE'RE MAINTAINING BALANCE, BUT...!

THE FUEL METER!

IT SHOULDN'T BE GOING DOWN LIKE THIS!

WE HAVE TO ASSUME THERE'S A HOLE IN OUR FUEL TANK!!!

We won't last until the airport!

Captain!! We need to make a forced landing on a road!!

HMM.

IT SEEMS YOUR ILLUSION HAS BEGUN TO TAKE EFFECT.

'TWOULD SEEM THE TERRORIST IS NO SORCERER—THOUGH THEY MAY BE INVOLVED WITH A MAJOR GROUP.

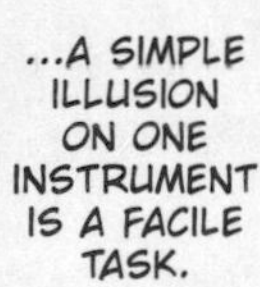

WHILE IT'S DIFFICULT TO HIJACK A PASSENGER PLANE FROM A DISTANCE...
...A SIMPLE ILLUSION ON ONE INSTRUMENT IS A FACILE TASK.

WHICH IS WHY YOU'RE HAVING THEM LAND ON AN EMPTIED ROAD RATHER THAN AN AIRPORT?
I HOPE LEAVING THE LANDING TO THEM IS THE RIGHT DECISION.
MY! WOULD YOU RATHER IT EXPLODE IN A MAJOR CITY?
WHAT IF THE PLANE WAS TO BREAK APART IN MIDAIR?

IN THAT CASE, WE'D NEED TO RECOVER AT LEAST THE INDEX.
IF IT'S JUST HER, I COULD CATCH HER BEFORE SHE HIT THE GROUND.
WITH THE BINDING SPELL I UTILIZED ON LIDVIA LORENZETTI.
...I SAY THIS FROM THE BOTTOM OF MY HEART—
I HOPE YOU DIE BEFORE YOUR TIME.

IN ANY CASE, THE ROYALS NEVER DID AGREE TO A DISCUSSION, DID THEY?
WITHOUT THE ROYALS HERE TO KEEP THE KNIGHTS IN CHECK, WE PURITANS ARE HELPLESS IN THE FACE OF YOUR TORMENT!
WAAAH...
HER MAJESTY IS A BUSY WOMAN.
WHO'S TORMENTING WHO HERE?

...NOW, ISN'T THAT JUST THE ODDEST THING?

ARCHBISHOP!!

EMERGENCY!

MAJOR INTERFERENCE FROM THE DIRECTION OF SCOTLAND!!

OUR ILLUSION HAS BEEN CUT OFF BY A THIRD PARTY!!

ZAWA
ZAWA (MURMUR)
WHAT'S GOING ON?
THAT WAS SCARY...
We now have an update for you all.

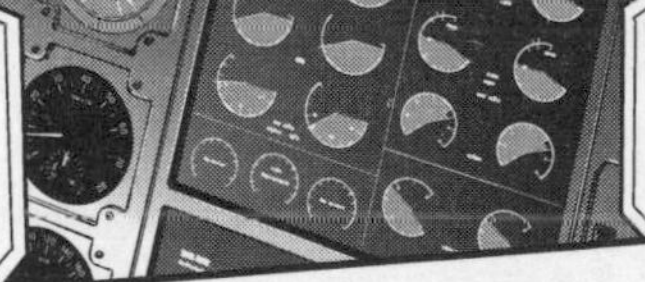
The earlier emergency alarm was due to an instrument malfunction.
This plane will be arriving in Edinburgh twenty minutes behind schedule.

...ALL THE READINGS ARE BACK TO NORMAL.
WHAT THE HELL HAPPENED?
WERE WE DAYDREAMING? ALL THREE OF US!?

TO THINK WE'D FACE INTER-FERENCE FROM WITHIN THE U.K.
I'M QUITE AWARE.
THIS FAILURE IS ON YOU.

JUST IN CASE, I'D LIKE TO PREPARE FOR ANY FUTURE DEVELOP-MENTS ON BOARD THE 365.
WHAT DO YOU NEED?

IN THAT CASE...

...JUST ONE TRANSPORT PLANE.

TOUMA! SHE SAYS WE CAN GO BACK TO OUR SEATS!
WHAT'S WRONG?
WHY DID HE MAKE HIS MOVE IN THE LAST HOUR OF THE FLIGHT?
HE WAS ON BOARD WITH US THE WHOLE TIME, WASN'T HE?
IF HE'D JUST DONE IT RIGHT AWAY, HE WOULDN'T HAVE PAN-ICKED AND SLIPPED UP.
PERHAPS HE WANTED TO CAUSE THE ISSUE IN BRITISH SKIES?
MAYBE HE WAS WAITING FOR BREAK-FAST!
BREAK-FAST...?
YOU'RE PROJECTING PRETTY HARD THERE.
THIS FLIGHT IS SLATED TO TRANSPORT EMERGENCY GOODS, LIKE MEDICINE, LIQUID FOOD, AND FRESH FOODSTUFFS.

......

THEY'RE STILL HERE.

IN THE HOLD!!

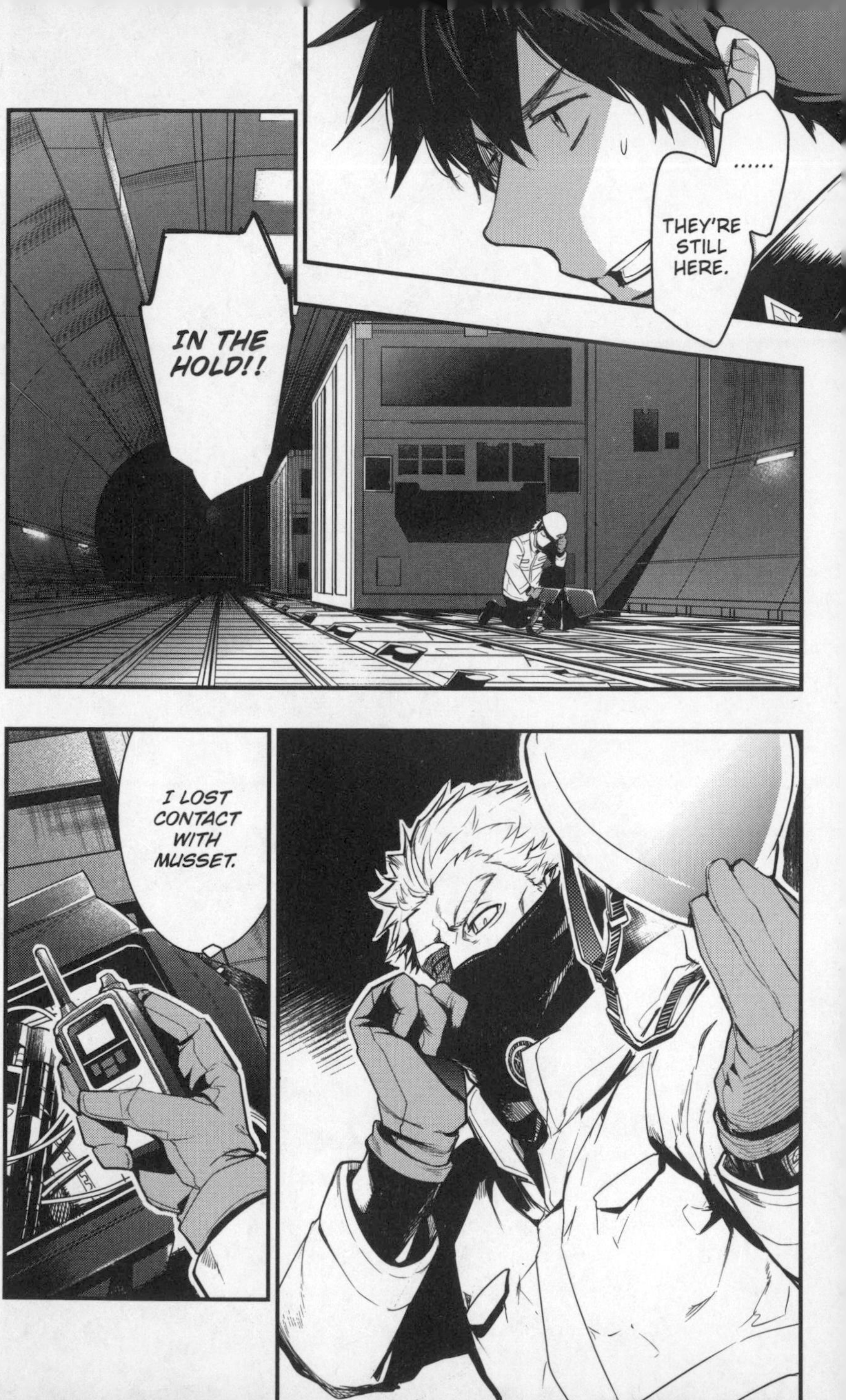

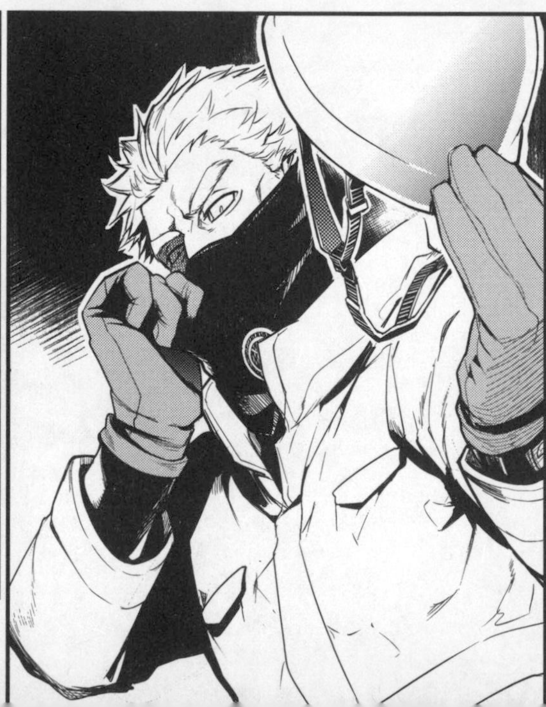

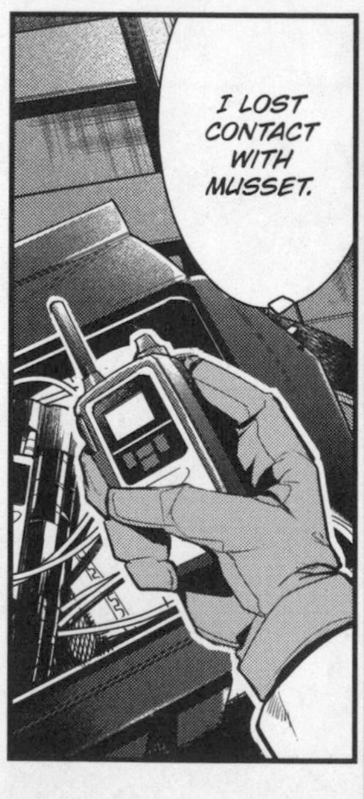
I LOST CONTACT WITH MUSSET.

SO NEGO-TIATIONS HAVE FAILED.
BUT AT THE VERY LEAST...
...I'LL BRING THIS PLANE DOWN!

CAN WE GET TO THE CARGO HOLD FROM THIS SIDE!?
Y-YES!
I'D NEED TO ASK THE CAPTAIN TO OPEN THE HATCH.
BUT...

...IF THE TERRORIST REALLY DOES HAVE A FRIEND HIDDEN IN A CONTAINER, THEY'LL SHOOT YOU THE MOMENT IT OPENS!
I CAN'T ALLOW A PAS-SENGER TO PUT HIMSELF IN THAT MUCH DANGER!!

I MEAN, WE'RE ALL IN DANGER ALREADY.
WHEN STUFF GETS LIKE THIS, TOUMA STOPS LISTENING TO PEOPLE.
HMM...
WELL, GETTING SHOT ISN'T REALLY SOMETHING I WANT TO DO.

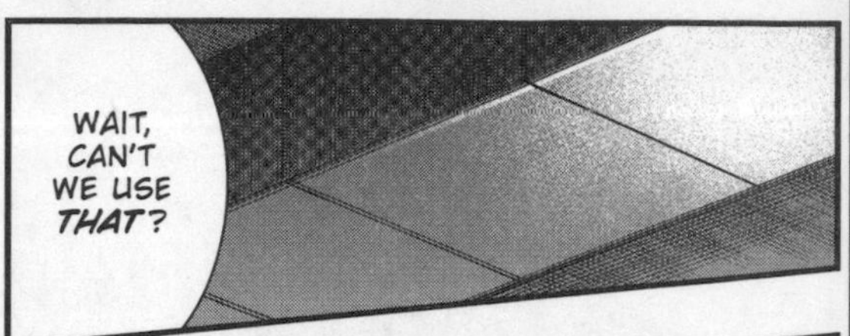

WAIT, CAN'T WE USE *THAT*?

THE VENTILATION DUCT?
IT'S NOT BIG ENOUGH FOR A PERSON.
THEY DON'T WORK LIKE IN THE MOVIES.
ACTUALLY, THAT'S FINE.

FIRST WE GOTTA PREPARE.

COULD YOU BRING ME SOME TEA?

...TEA, SIR?

YEAH.

AND MAKE IT AS HOT AS YOU POSSIBLY CAN!

BON (KMMP)

...IT'S TIME.

BOKON (KRRMP)
BOKON
BAN (BANG)
BAN

!?
IS THIS...

'SUP, TERROR-IST?
...TEA ...??
BA (WHMP)
SHA (SHHHHK)

GA (GRAB)

AGHGHGHHHH!!!

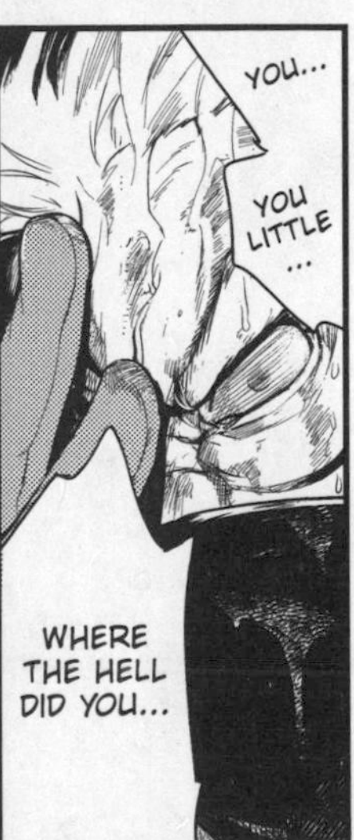

YOU...
YOU LITTLE ...
WHERE THE HELL DID YOU...

DIDN'T NOTICE THE SOUND OVER THE GUNSHOTS, HUH?
I CAME IN THROUGH THE HATCH.
DAMN IT!

LOOK AT THIS!!
A DETONATOR!?
FRANCE LOST SO MUCH FROM THE EUROTUNNEL EXPLOSION...!
NOW THEY'LL FEEL THE SAME PAIN—
THE PAIN OF ISOLATION AS THEIR AIR LANES ARE CUT OFF JUST LIKE THEIR LAND ROUTE!
DON'T!

THE U.K. LOST A LOT FROM THE TUNNEL EXPLOSION TOO, DIDN'T THEY!?
YOU'RE JUST TRYING TO SELFISHLY PIN THE BLAME ON WHATEVER COUNTRY YOU WANT! DON'T GET INNOCENT PEOPLE INVOLVED!

...SELF-ISH?

THEY'RE THE ONES BEING SELFISH... THEY'RE THE ONES REFUSING OUR ATTEMPTS AT NEGOTIA-TION!

IF THE PLAN TO USE THE DEFECT IN THE SAFETIES HAD SUCCEEDED...WE COULD HAVE SOLD THIS INTEL AND MADE OUR GROUP FAMOUS...SO NOW THAT IT'S COME TO THIS, WE'RE LEFT WITH ONLY OUR LAST RESORT.

IF NOTHING ELSE!!

I'M TAKING THIS PLANE DOWN!!!

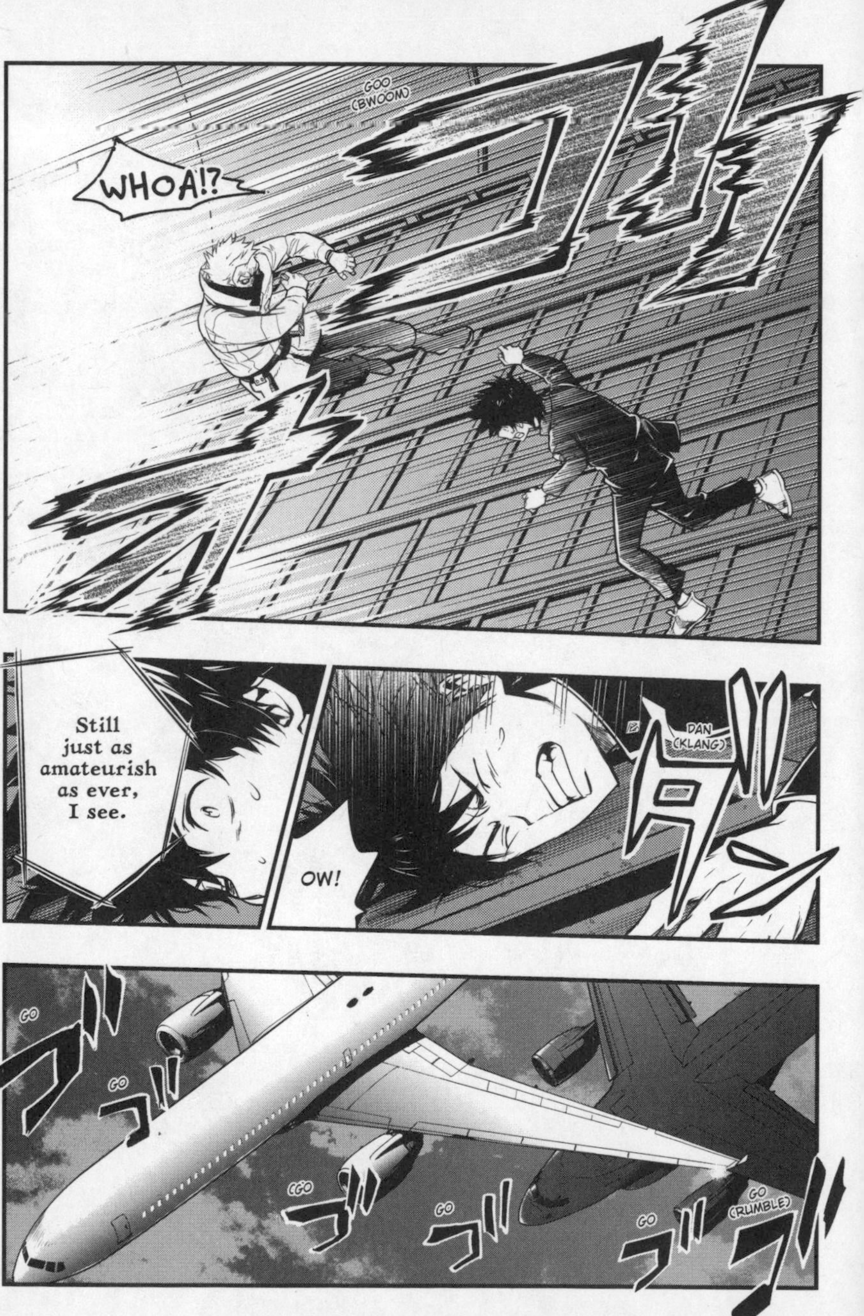

GOO
(BWOOM)
WHOA!?

DAN
(KLANG)
OW!
Still just as amateurish as ever, I see.

GO
(RUMBLE)
GO
GO
GO
GO
GO

YOU'RE PUTTING EVERYONE ELSE IN DANGER...

...BY HESITATING TO KILL.

STIYL!

JU
(ZHT)

BYUOOOOO (WHOOORRRRRRR)
ビュオオオオオオ
ZU (SHHH) ZU
ズズ
SHIT!
I'LL GET SUCKED OUT!
BITAA (WHUNK)
ビタァ

GOKI (CRACK)

BOKI (KRIK)

BUCHI (KRCHHH)

GGGH-GHGH-GHH!

Look at that.

A perfect plug for you.

Ten minutes until Edinburgh Airport.

He should live until then. Probably.

BRUTAL.

...SERI-
OUSLY.
I WISH YOU WERE PREPARED TO DO AT LEAST THIS MUCH.
YOU ARE SUPPOSED TO BE RESPONSIBLE FOR HER, AFTER ALL.

Breaking news.

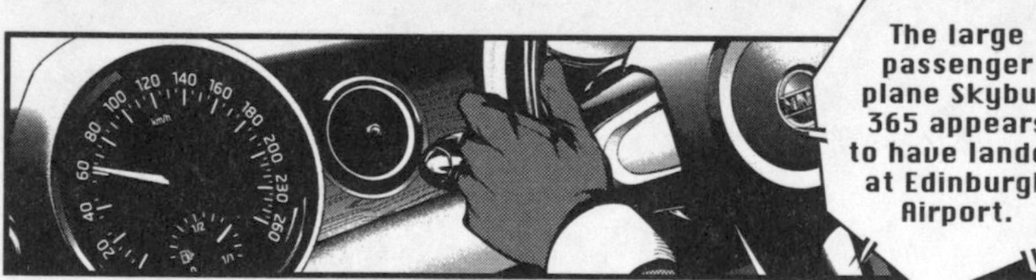

The large passenger plane Skybus 365 appears to have landed at Edinburgh Airport.

...LOOKS LIKE THAT PLANE LANDED SAFELY.

BUT ONLY BECAUSE THEY GOT A TRANSPORT WITH STEALTH TECHNOLOGY FROM ACADEMY CITY TO HELP, RIGHT?
GET YOUR TAIL OUT OF MY FACE, LESSER...

IF YOU DON'T PUT IT AWAY, I'M PULLING IT OUT.
BIN (YANK)
AHHHH!?
BAYLOUPE!! ARE YOU ON EDGE BEFORE THE MISSION!?
I MEAN, WE CAN'T BE LOST ON A ROAD LIKE THIS, RIGHT?
THE SCENERY LITERALLY NEVER CHANGES, HUH?

LAN-CIS?
ARE YOU SURE THIS IS THE RIGHT ROAD?

SHAKING BECAUSE OF MANA YOU MADE FOR YOURSELF...
WHAT ABOUT REFINING LIFE FORCE INTO MANA MAKES THAT HAPPEN ANYWAY?
AHH, FWAH!

P-PLEASE STOP... IT TICKLES...
WHEN-EVER I GET MANA...
M-MY BODY, IT...
EE HEE HEE HEE!
......

HEY, YOU TWO IN THE BACK.
IS THE SKITH-BLATHNIR READY?

YOU MEAN THE CASES?
I'M DONE ADJUSTING ALL FOUR OF THEM.
GOOD WORK.

WE'RE ABOUT TO TAKE THE UNITED KINGDOM...

...AND TEAR IT APART AT THE SEAMS.

A CERTAIN MAGICAL INDEX 27 END

Preview

AT THE REQUEST OF THE ENGLISH PURITAN CHURCH...

...I'VE COME TO WELCOME YOU TWO AS THE PRIESTESS OF THE REBORN AMAKUSA-STYLE CROSSIST CHURCH.

......WILLIAM...
TOUMA AND INDEX FINALLY ARRIVE IN THE UNITED KINGDOM...

KNIGHT LEADER.

SO YOU'VE COME.

TO THINK YOU WOULD ADMINISTER IT BY LETTING IT HANG FROM YOUR HEAD LIKE THAT.
THE SECRET ARTS OF ASIA CONTINUE TO ASTONISH.
GARURURURU (GRRRRRR)

JUST WHAT FATE AWAITS THEM...
HER MAJESTY ELIZARD, THE QUEEN OF BRITAIN.
...AFTER THEIR AUDIENCE WITH THE QUEEN...!?

A Certain Magical Index

Volume 28

Please look forward to it!

azuma Kamachi
iyotaka Haimura
Chuya Kogino

Lettering: Phil Christie

Yen Press
150 West 30th Street, 19th Floor
New York, NY 10001

Visit us at yenpress.com
facebook.com/yenpress
twitter.com/yenpress
yenpress.tumblr.com
instagram.com/yenpress

First Yen Press Edition: August 2023
Edited by Yen Press Editorial: Thomas McAlister, Carl Li
Designed by Yen Press Design: Liz Parlett

Library of Congress Control Number: 2015373809

ISBNs: 978-1-9753-7149-4 (paperback)
978-1-9753-7150-0 (ebook)

10 9 8 7 6 5 4 3 2 1

WOR

Printed in the United States of America